Reflections on
Humanae Vitae

Reflections on *Humanae Vitae*

Conjugal Morality and Spirituality

JOHN PAUL II

**Preface by
Rev. Msgr. Donald W. Wuerl**
*St. Paul's Seminary
Pittsburgh, Pennsylvania*

ST. PAUL EDITIONS

Reprinted with permission of *L'Osservatore Romano*, English Edition.

Library of Congress Cataloging in Publication Data

John Paul II, Pope, 1920-
    Reflections on "Humanae vitae."

    1. Catholic Church. Pope (1963-1978: Paul VI).
Humanae vitae—Addresses, essays, lectures. 2. Birth
control—Religious aspects—Catholic Church—Addresses,
essays, lectures. 3. Catholic Church—Doctrines—
Addresses, essays, lectures. 4. Marriage—Religious
aspects—Catholic Church—Addresses, essays, lectures.
I. Daughters of St. Paul. II. Title.

HQ766.3.C37J64   1984   241'.66   84-28625

ISBN 0-8198-6409-9 c.
       0-8198-6410-2 p.

Printed in the U.S.A. by the Daughters of St. Paul
50 St. Paul's Ave., Boston, MA 02130

The Daughters of St. Paul are an international congregation of women religious serving the Church with the communications media.

CONTENTS

Preface

In his recent addresses on human life our Holy Father, Pope John Paul II, focuses attention on the Church's abiding concern for human life. The roots of this Catholic tradition take us far back into Sacred Scripture. The author of Genesis tells us that "God formed man in the image of himself," and then "he breathed into his nostrils a breath of life and thus man became a living being." Scripture scholars continue to see the "breath of God" as the life-giving spirit given by God in a unique manner to all human beings. To destroy this life is, of course, a terrible act. The reason for this is that God's spirit, God's *"ruah,"* as the Old Testament puts it, comes to inhabit the human being. Human dignity exists in the Bible because humans possess God's life, God's spirit. We have this from God Himself. With this initial thrust the Judaeo-Christian tradition records throughout the pages of the Sacred Scriptures the uniqueness of life and the reverence all attach to it. After a detailed setting down of the old law in Deuteronomy, the lawgiver calls attention to the choice that must be made—to accept the law or reject it. "See, today I set before you life and prosperity, death and disaster." The quotation runs on: "To love God is to choose life. I call heaven and earth to witness against you today. I set before you life and death, a blessing and a curse. Choose life, then, so that you and your descendants may live in the love of the Lord your God, obeying his voice, clinging to him, for in this your life consists" (Dt. 30:19-20).

Throughout the pages of the old covenant the Lord is revealed as the Lord of life. The person who shares in this gift must be first and foremost the custodian of life. "I will demand an account of your life.... I will demand an account of every human's life from his fellow humans" (Gn. 9:5). As for the life of children, the Old Testament books spoke in terms of their blessing. The first blessing on a human was: "Be fruitful, multiply and fill the earth" (Gn. 1:28). For the prophet Isaiah, this God-given blessing establishes a personal relationship between God and the person even before the person sees the light of day. "The Lord God called me before I was born, from my mother's womb he pronounced my name" (Is. 49:1). The prophet Jeremiah states the same idea: "Before I formed you in the womb I knew you, before you came to birth I consecrated you: I have appointed you as a prophet to the nations" (Jer. 1:5).

Nor is the New Testament silent on life as God's most cherished gift to humans. John tells us that Christ came "so that they might have life and have it to the full" (Jn. 10:10). John sees human life as the necessary reality for transformation into a life that will know no end. For him, human life is sacred, but is called to be divine life. His use of the sequence—faith, light, life (Jn. 12:35-36)—reflects this view. Such a view makes sense only when one starts with the God-given gift of life that all humans share and that some by faith perfect into everlasting life.

In fact, the whole perspective of the new order—the new covenant of God the Son—is that human life is perfected and made divine. Matthew outlines in the several chapters that make up the Sermon on the Mount some of the essential attitudes that are the result of this new perspective. The Gospel insists on the vision of humans as eventual citizens of heaven. The balance is set between the works of this world and those directed to the life to come. The background is always human life seen as potentially divine and eternal. The Sermon on the Mount requires that the believer see his fellow human's dignity. This dignity comes from God, resides in the human and is held sacred because of our ultimate goal, which is union with God.

Today the whole question of the value of human life and the proper context within which it should be seen is debated. For the time being the contraceptionists have won their battle. The fight has now moved to abortion. Many see in today's legislation a victory for the abortionists. From abortion, if another victory is completely won, we stand at the mercy of euthanasia and mass class elimination. The Church has always viewed human life in its continuity from conception to death. The decision of any to interrupt that life at any point is an unwarranted intrusion into a realm over which humans do not possess dominion.

Human life is sacred. But the revealed fact that this life is not destroyed merely changed makes our life all the more holy.

It is this awareness that permeates the talks of Pope John Paul II which have been so carefully collected here by the Daughters of St. Paul for the benefit of all the living.

We should all be grateful to our Holy Father for reminding us of something so essential, and we should be equally appreciative of the efforts of the Daughters of St. Paul to make these words so readily available.

Rev. Msgr. Donald W. Wuerl
St. Paul's Seminary
Pittsburgh, Pennsylvania

Morality of the Marriage Act Determined by the Nature of the Act and of the Subjects

General audience of July 11, 1984.

1. The reflections we have thus far made on human love in the divine plan* would be in some way incomplete if we did not try to see their concrete application in the sphere of marital and family morality. We want to take this further step that will bring us to the conclusion of our now long journey, under the guidance of an important recent pronouncement of the Magisterium, the Encyclical *Humanae vitae*, which Pope Paul VI published in July of 1968. We will reread this significant document in the light of the conclusions we have reached in examining the initial divine plan and the words of Christ which refer to it.

---

*Here the Holy Father refers to his series of talks on the redemption of the body and the sacramentality of marriage which have been published by the Daughters of St. Paul under the titles **Original Unity of Man and Woman** and **Blessed Are the Pure of Heart**, with a third volume in preparation.

FROM *HUMANAE VITAE*

2. "The Church teaches as absolutely required that in any use whatever of marriage there must be no impairment of its natural capacity to procreate human life..." (HV 11). "This particular doctrine, often expounded by the Magisterium of the Church, is based on the inseparable connection, established by God, which man on his own initiative may not break, between the unitive significance and the procreative significance which are both inherent to the marriage act" (HV 12).

3. The considerations I am about to make concern particularly the passage of the Encyclical *Humanae vitae* that deals with the "two *significances* of the marriage act" and their "inseparable connection." I do not intend to present a commentary on the whole encyclical, but rather to illustrate and examine one of its passages. From the point of view of the doctrine contained in the quoted document, that passage has a central significance. At the same time, that passage is closely connected with our previous reflections on *marriage in its dimension as a (sacramental) sign.*

Since, as I said, it is a central passage of the encyclical, it is obvious that it constitutes a very important part of its whole structure: its analysis, therefore, must direct us toward the various components of that structure, even if it is not our intention to comment on the entire text.

A PROMISED FIDELITY

4. In the reflections on the sacramental sign, it has already been said several times that it is based on the *"language of the body" reread in truth*. It concerns a truth once affirmed at the beginning of the marriage when the newlyweds, promising each other "to be always faithful... and to love and honor each other all the days of their life," become ministers of marriage as a sacrament of the Church.

It concerns, then, a truth that is, so to speak, always newly affirmed. In fact, the man and the woman, living in the marriage "until death," repropose uninterruptedly, in a certain sense, that sign that they made—through the liturgy of the sacrament—on their wedding day.

The aforementioned words of Pope Paul VI's encyclical concern that moment in the common life of the spouses when both, joining each other in the marriage act, become, according to the biblical expression, "one body" (Gn. 2:24). Precisely *at such a moment so rich in significance,* it is also especially important that the "language of the body" be reread in truth. This reading becomes the indispensable condition for acting in truth, that is, for behaving in accordance with the value and the moral norm.

ADEQUATE FOUNDATION

5. The encyclical not only recalls this norm, but also seeks to give it adequate foundation. In order to clarify more completely that "inseparable connection, established by God,... between the unitive significance and the procreative significance of the marriage act," Paul VI writes in the next sentence: "The reason is that the marriage act, because of its fundamental structure, while it unites husband and wife in the closest intimacy, also brings into operation laws written into the actual nature of man and of woman for the generation of new life" (HV 12).

We note that in the previous sentence, the text just quoted deals above all with the "significance" and in the following sentence with the "fundamental structure" (that is, the nature) of marital relations. Defining that "fundamental structure," the text refers to "laws written into the actual nature of man and of woman."

The passage from the sentence expressing the moral norm to the sentence which explains and justifies it is especially significant. The encyclical leads one to seek the foundation for the norm which determines the morality of the acts of the man and the woman in the marriage act, in the nature of this very act, and more deeply still, in the nature of the subjects themselves who are performing the act.

TWO SIGNIFICANCES

6. In this way, the "fundamental structure" (that is, the nature) of the marriage act constitutes the necessary basis for an adequate reading and discovery of the two significances that must by carried over into the conscience and the decisions of the acting parties, and also the necessary basis for establishing the adequate relationship of these significances, that is, their inseparable connection. Since "the marriage act..."—at the same time—"unites husband and wife in the closest intimacy" and, together, "makes them capable of generating new life," and both the one and the other happen "through the fundamental structure," then it follows that the human person (with the necessity proper to reason, logical necessity) "must" read at the same time the "twofold significance of the marriage act" and also the "inseparable connection between the unitive significance and the procreative significance of the marriage act."

Here we are dealing with nothing other than reading the "language of the body" in truth, as has been said many times in our previous biblical analyses. The moral norm, constantly taught by the Church in this sphere, and recalled and reconfirmed by Paul VI in his encyclical, arises from the reading of the "language of the body" *in truth*.

It is a question here of the *truth* first *in the ontological dimension* ("fundamental structure") and then—as a result—in the *subjective and psychological dimension* ("significance"). The text of the encyclical stresses that in the case in question we are dealing with a norm of the natural law.

The Norm of *Humanae Vitae* Arises from the Natural Law and Revealed Order

General audience of July 18, 1984.

1. In the Encyclical *Humanae vitae* we read: "The Church, in urging men to the observance of the precepts of the natural law, which it interprets by its constant doctrine, teaches as absolutely required that in any use whatever of marriage there must be no impairment of its natural capacity to procreate human life" (HV 11).

At the same time this same text considers and even puts emphasis on the subjective and psychological dimension when it speaks of the "significance," and precisely of the "two significances of the marital act."

The "significance" becomes known with the rereading of the (ontological) truth of the object.

Through this rereading, the (ontological) truth enters, so to speak, into the cognitive dimension: subjective and psychological.

Humanae vitae seems to draw our attention especially to this latter dimension. This is confirmed, among other ways, indirectly, also by the following sentence: "We believe that our contemporaries are particularly capable of seeing that this teaching is in harmony with human reason" (HV 12).

THE MORAL NORM
AND ITS REASON

2. That "reasonable character" concerns not only the truth of the ontological dimension, namely, that which corresponds to the fundamental structure of the marital act, but it concerns also the same truth in the subjective and psychological dimension, that is to say, the correct understanding of the intimate structure of the marital act, that is, the adequate rereading of the significances corresponding to this structure and of their inseparable connection, in view of a morally right behavior. Herein lies precisely the moral norm and the corresponding regulation of human acts in the sphere of sexuality. In this sense we say that the moral norm is identified with the rereading, in truth, of the "language of the body."

3. The Encyclical *Humanae vitae*, therefore, contains the moral norm and its reason, or at least an examination of what constitutes the reason for the norm. Moreover, since in the norm the moral value is expressed in a binding way, it follows that acts in conformity with the norm are morally right, while acts contrary to it are intrinsically illicit. The author of the encyclical stresses that this norm belongs to the "natural law," that is to say, it is in accordance with reason as such. The Church teaches this norm, although it is not formally (that is, literally) expressed in Sacred Scripture, and it does this in the conviction that the interpretation of the precepts of natural law belongs to the competence of the Magisterium.

However, we can say more. Even if the moral law, formulated in this way in the Encyclical *Humanae vitae*, is not found literally in Sacred Scripture, nonetheless, from the fact that it is contained in tradition and—as Pope Paul VI writes—has been "very often expounded by the Magisterium" (HV 12) to the faithful, it follows that this norm is in accordance with the sum total of revealed doctrine contained in biblical sources (cf. HV 4).

REVEALED BY GOD

4. It is a question here not only of the sum total of the moral doctrine contained in Sacred

Scripture, of its essential premises and the general character of its content, but of that fuller context to which we have previously dedicated numerous analyses when speaking about the "theology of the body."

Precisely against the background of this full context it becomes evident that the above-mentioned moral norm belongs not only to the natural moral law, but also to the *moral order revealed by God:* also from this point of view, it could not be different, but solely what is handed down by Tradition and the Magisterium and, in our days, the Encyclical *Humanae vitae* as a modern document of this Magisterium.

Paul VI writes: "We believe that our contemporaries are particularly capable of seeing that this teaching is in harmony with human reason" (HV 12). We can add: They are capable also of seeing its profound conformity with all that is transmitted by Tradition stemming from biblical sources. The bases of this conformity are to be sought especially in biblical anthropology. Moreover, we know the significance that anthropology has for ethics, that is, for moral doctrine. It seems to be totally reasonable to look precisely in the "theology of the body" for the foundation of the truth of the norms that concern the fundamental problematic of man as "body": "the two will become one flesh" (Gn. 2:24).

REREAD AND REFLECT

5. The norm of the Encyclical *Humanae vitae* concerns all men, insofar as it is a norm of the natural law and is based on conformity with human reason (when, it is understood, human reason is seeking truth). All the more does it concern all believers and members of the Church, since the reasonable character of this norm indirectly finds confirmation and solid support in the sum total of the "theology of the body." From this point of view we have spoken in previous analyses about the "ethos" of the redemption of the body.

The norm of the natural law, based on this "ethos," finds not only a new expression, but also a fuller anthropological and ethical foundation in the word of the Gospel and in the purifying and corroborating action of the Holy Spirit.

These are all reasons why every believer and especially every theologian should reread and ever more deeply understand the moral doctrine of the encyclical in this complete context.

The reflections we have been making here for some time constitute precisely an attempt at this rereading.

Importance of Harmonizing Human Love with Respect for Life

General audience of July 25, 1984.

1. Today we continue our reflections which are directed toward linking the Encyclical *Humanae vitae* to our whole treatment of the theology of the body.

This encyclical is not limited to recalling the moral norm concerning conjugal life, reconfirming this norm in the face of new circumstances. Paul VI, in making a pronouncement with the authentic Magisterium through the encyclical (1968), had before his eyes the authoritative statement of the Second Vatican Council contained in the Constitution *Gaudium et spes* (1965).

The encyclical is not only found to be along the lines of the Council's teaching, but it also constitutes the development and completion of the questions contained there, particularly regarding the question of the "harmony of human love with respect for life." On this point, we read in *Gaudium et spes* the following words: "The Church issues the reminder that a true contradiction cannot exist between the divine laws pertaining to the transmission of life and those pertaining to the fostering of authentic conjugal love" (GS 51).

THE MORAL NORM DOES NOT CONTRADICT REASON

2. The pastoral constitution of Vatican II excludes any "true contradiction" whatsoever in the normative order which on his part Paul VI confirms by seeking at the same time to shed light on that "noncontradiction," and thus to justify the respective moral norm by demonstrating its conformity to reason.

Nevertheless, *Humanae vitae* speaks not so much of the *"noncontradiction"* in the normative order as of the *"inseparable connection"* between the transmission of life and authentic marital love from the point of view of the "two significances of the conjugal act: the unitive significance and the procreative significance" (HV 12), with which we have already dealt.

3. We could pause for some time here analyzing the norm itself, but the character of

both the one and the other document leads rather to reflections that are, at least indirectly, pastoral. In fact, *Gaudium et spes* is a pastoral constitution, and Paul VI's encyclical—with its doctrinal value—tends to have the same orientation. In fact, it is intended to be *a response to the questions of modern man*. These questions are of a demographic nature, and consequently of a socio-economic and political nature, in relation to the population increase throughout the world. They are questions that begin from the field of particular sciences, and at the same rate are questions of modern moralists (theologians-moralists). They are above all questions of spouses which are already found at the center of attention in the conciliar constitution and are taken up again in the encyclical with all the desirable precision. In fact, we read there: "Granted the conditions of life today and taking into account the relevance of married love to the harmony and mutual fidelity of husband and wife, would it not be right to review the moral norms in force till now, especially when it is felt that these can be observed only with the gravest difficulty, sometimes only by heroic effort?" (HV 3)

PASTORAL ARGUMENTS

4. In the above text it is evident with what solicitude the encyclical's author tries to face the questions of modern man in all their import. The

relevance of these questions presupposes a response that is proportionately thought out and profound. If, therefore, on the one hand it is right to expect a keenly sensitive treatment of the norm, on the other hand it can also be expected that no small weight be given to the pastoral arguments, more directly concerning the life of man in the concrete, of precisely those who are posing the questions mentioned in the beginning.

Paul VI always had these people before his eyes. Evidence of this, among other things, is the following passage of *Humanae vitae:* "The teaching of the Church regarding the right ordering of the increase of a man's family is a promulgation of the law of God Himself. And yet there is no doubt that to many it may appear not merely difficult but even impossible to observe. Now it is true that like all good things which are outstanding for their nobility and for the benefits which they confer on men, so this law demands from individual men and women, from families and from human society a resolute purpose and great endurance. Indeed it cannot be observed unless God comes to their help with that grace by which the good will of men is sustained and strengthened. But to those who consider this matter diligently it will indeed be evident that this endurance enhances man's dignity and confers benefits on human society" (HV 20).

RULE OF UNDERSTANDING

5. At this point there is no more mention of the normative "noncontradiction" but rather of the "possibility of observing the divine law," that is, of an argument that is at least indirectly pastoral. The fact that the law must be "possible" to observe belongs directly to the very nature of law and is therefore included in the framework of the "normative noncontradiction." Nevertheless the "possibility," understood as the "feasibility" of the norm, belongs also to the practical and pastoral sphere. In the text quoted, my Predecessor speaks, precisely, from this point of view.

6. We can here arrive at a consideration: the fact that the whole biblical background, called "theology of the body," offers us, even though indirectly, the confirmation of the truth of the moral norm contained in *Humanae vitae,* prepares us to consider more deeply the practical and pastoral aspects of the problem in its entirety. Were not the principles and general presuppositions of the "theology of the body" all taken from the answers Christ gave to the questions of His actual audience? And are not Paul's texts—as, for example, in the Letter to the Corinthians—a small manual on the problems of the moral life of Christ's first followers? And in these texts we certainly find that "rule of

understanding" which seems so indispensable in the face of the problems treated in *Humanae vitae* and which is present in this encyclical.

Whoever believes that the Council and the encyclical do not sufficiently take into account the difficulties present in concrete life does not understand the pastoral concern that was at the origin of those documents. Pastoral concern means the search for the true good of man, a promotion of the values engraved in his person by God; that is, it means observing that "rule of understanding" which is directed to the ever clearer discovery of God's plan for human love, in the certitude that the only true good of the human person consists in fulfilling this divine plan.

One could say that, precisely in the name of the aforementioned "rule of understanding," the Council posed the question of the "harmony of human love with respect for life" (GS 51), and the Encyclical *Humanae vitae* then not only recalls the moral norms that are binding in this area, but is also fully concerned with the problem of the "possibility of observing the divine law."

The present reflections on the nature of the document *Humanae vitae* prepare us to deal then with the theme of "responsible parenthood."

Responsible Parenthood

General audience of August 1, 1984.

1. For today we have chosen the theme of "responsible parenthood" in the light of the Constitution *Gaudium et spes* and of the Encyclical *Humanae vitae.*

The Council document, in treating of the subject, limits itself to recalling the basic premises; the papal document, however, goes further, giving to these premises a more concrete content.

The Council text reads as follows: "When it is a question of harmonizing married love with the responsible transmission of life, it is not enough to take only the good intention and the evaluation of motives into account; the objective criteria must be used, criteria drawn from the nature of the human person and human action, criteria which respect the total meaning of mutual self-giving and human procreation in the context of true love; all this is possible only if the virtue of married chastity is seriously practiced" (GS 51).

The Council adds: "In questions of birth regulation the sons of the Church, faithful to these principles, are forbidden to use methods disapproved of by the teaching authority of the Church" (GS 51).

RULED BY CONSCIENCE

2. Before the passage quoted, the Council teaches that married couples "shall fulfill their role with a sense of human and Christian responsibility and the formation of correct judgments through docile respect for God" (GS 50). This involves "common reflection and effort; it also involves a consideration of their own good and the good of their children already born or yet to come, an ability to read the signs of the times and of their own situation on the material and spiritual level, and finally, an estimation of the good of the family, of society and of the Church" (GS 50).

At this point there follow words of particular importance to determine with greater precision the moral character of "responsible parenthood." We read: "It is the married couple themselves who must in the last analysis arrive at these judgments before God" (GS 50).

And it continues: "Married people should realize that in their behavior they may not simply follow their own fancy but must be ruled by conscience—and conscience ought to be conformed to the law of God in the light of the teaching authority of the Church, which is the authentic interpreter of divine law. For the divine law throws light on the meaning of married love, protects it and leads it to truly human fulfillment" (GS 50).

3. The Council document, in limiting itself to recalling the necessary premises for responsible parenthood, has set them out in a completely unambiguous manner, clarifying the constitutive elements of such parenthood, that is, the mature judgment of the personal conscience in relationship to the divine law, authentically interpreted by the Magisterium of the Church.

TRUE CONJUGAL LOVE

4. The Encyclical *Humanae vitae,* basing itself on the same premises, goes further and offers concrete indications. This is seen, first of all, in the way of defining "responsible parenthood" (HV 10). Paul VI seeks to clarify this concept by considering its various aspects and excluding beforehand its reduction to one of the "partial aspects, as is done by those who speak exclusively of birth control." From the very beginning, indeed, Paul VI is guided in his reasoning by an integral concept of man (cf. HV 7) and of conjugal love (cf. HV 8, 9).

UNDER DIFFERENT ASPECTS

5. One can speak of responsibility in the exercise of the function of parenthood under different aspects. Thus he writes: "In relation to the biological processes involved, responsible parenthood is to be understood as the knowledge and observance of their specific functions. Human intelligence discovers in the faculty of procreating life, the biological laws which involve human personality" (HV 10). If, on the other hand, we examine "the innate drives and emotions of man, responsible parenthood expresses the domination which reason and will must exert over them" (HV 10).

Taking for granted the above-mentioned intra-personal aspects and adding to them the "economic and social conditions," those are considered "to exercise responsible parenthood who prudently and generously decide to have a large family, or who, for serious reasons and with due respect to the moral law, choose to have no more children for the time being or even for an indeterminate period" (HV 10).

From this it follows that the concept of "responsible parenthood" contains the disposition not merely to avoid "a further birth" but also to increase the family in accordance with the criteria of prudence. In this light in which the question of "responsible parenthood" must be examined and decided, there is always of paramount importance "the objective moral order instituted by God, the order of which a right conscience is the true interpreter" (HV 10).

6. The commitment to responsible parenthood requires that husband and wife, "keeping a right order of priorities, recognize their own duties towards God, themselves, their families and human society" (HV 10). One cannot therefore speak of "acting arbitrarily." On the contrary the married couple "must act in conformity with God's creative intention" (HV 10). Beginning with this principle the encyclical bases its reasoning on the "intimate structure of the conjugal act" and on "the inseparable connection of the two significances of the conjugal act" (cf. HV 12), as was already stated previously. The relative principle of conjugal morality is, therefore, fidelity to the divine plan manifested in the "intimate structure of the conjugal act" and in the "inseparable connection of the two significances of the conjugal act."

Faithfulness to the Divine Plan in the Transmission of Life

General audience of August 8, 1984.

1. We said previously that the principle of conjugal morality, taught by the Church (Second Vatican Council, Paul VI), is the criterion of faithfulness to the divine plan.

In conformity with this principle the Encyclical *Humanae vitae* clearly distinguishes between a morally illicit method of birth regulation or, more precisely, of the regulation of fertility, and one that is morally correct.

In the first place "the direct interruption of the generative process already begun ('abortion') is morally wrong" (HV 14), likewise "direct sterilization" and "any action, which either before, at the moment of, or after sexual intercourse, is specifically intended to prevent procreation" (HV 14)—therefore, all contraceptive means. It is however morally lawful to have "recourse to the infertile periods" (HV 16): "If therefore there are reasonable grounds for spacing births, arising from the physical or psychological conditions of husband or wife, or from external circumstances, the Church teaches that then married people may take advantage of the natural cycles immanent in the reproductive system and use their marriage at precisely those times that are infertile, and in this way control birth without offending moral principles..." (HV 16).

NATURAL REGULATION VERSUS CONTRACEPTION

2. The encyclical emphasizes particularly that "between the two cases there is an essential difference" (HV 16), and therefore a difference of an ethical nature: "in the first case married couples rightly use a facility provided them by nature; in the other case, they obstruct the natural development of the generative process" (HV 16).

From this there derive two actions that are ethically different, indeed, even opposed: the natural regulation of fertility is morally correct; contraception is not morally correct. This essential difference between the two actions (modes of acting) concerns their intrinsic ethical character, even though my Predecessor Paul VI states that "in each case married couples, for acceptable reasons, are both perfectly clear in their intention to avoid children," and he even writes: "that they mean to make sure that none will be born." (HV 16). In these words the document admits that even those who make use of contraceptive practices can be motivated by "acceptable reasons"; however, this *does not change the moral character which is based on the very structure of the conjugal act as such.*

MORAL AND PASTORAL DIMENSIONS

3. It might be observed at this point that married couples who have recourse to the natural regulation of fertility, might do so without the valid reasons spoken of above. This, however, is a separate ethical problem, when one treats of the moral sense of "responsible parenthood."

Supposing that the reasons for deciding not to procreate are morally correct, there remains the *moral* problem of the manner of acting in this case, and this is expressed in an act which —according to the doctrine of the Church contained in the encyclical—possesses its own intrinsic moral qualification, either positive or negative. The first one, positive, corresponds to the "natural" regulation of fertility; the second, negative, corresponds to "artificial contraception."

4. The whole of the previous discussion is summed up in the exposition of the doctrine contained in *Humanae vitae,* by pointing out its

normative and at the same time its pastoral character. In the normative dimension it is a question of making more precise and clear the moral principles of action; in the pastoral dimension it is a question especially of pointing out the possibility of acting in accordance with these principles ("the possibility of the observance of the divine law," HV 20).

We should dwell on the interpretation of the content of the encyclical. To this end one must view that content, that normative-pastoral ensemble, in the light of the theology of the body as it emerges from the analysis of the biblical texts.

5. The theology of the body is not merely a theory, but rather a specific, evangelical, Christian pedagogy of the body. This derives from the character of the Bible, and especially of the Gospel which, as the message of salvation, reveals man's true good, for the purpose of modeling—according to the measure of this good—man's earthly life in the perspective of the hope of the future world.

The Encyclical *Humanae vitae,* following this line, responds to the question about the true good of man as a person, as male and female; about that which corresponds to the dignity of man and woman when one treats of the important problem of the transmission of life by married couples.

To this we shall devote further reflection.

The Church's Position on the Transmission of Life

General audience of August 22, 1984.

1. What is the essence of the Church's doctrine concerning the transmission of life in the conjugal community, of that doctrine of which we are reminded by the Pastoral Constitution of the Council, *Gaudium et spes,* and by the Encyclical *Humanae vitae* of Pope Paul VI?

The problem consists in maintaining an adequate relationship between what is defined as "domination...of the forces of nature" (HV 2), and the "mastery of self" (HV 21) which is indispensable for the human person. Modern man shows a tendency to transfer the methods proper to the former to those of the latter. "Man has made stupendous progress in the domination and rational organization of the forces of nature," we read in the encyclical, "to the point that he is endeavoring to extend this control over every aspect of his own life—over his body, over his mind and emotions, over his social life, and even over the laws that regulate the transmission of life" (HV 2).

This extension of the sphere of the means of "domination of the forces of nature" menaces the human person for whom the method of "self-mastery" is and remains specific. The mastery of self, in fact, corresponds to the fundamental constitution of the person: it is indeed a "natural" method. On the contrary, the resort to "artificial means" destroys the constitutive dimension of the person; it deprives man of the subjectivity proper to him and makes him an object of manipulation.

THE MEANING OF
THE "LANGUAGE OF THE BODY"

2. The human body is not merely an organism of sexual reactions, but it is, at the same time, the means of expressing the entire man, the person, which reveals itself by means of the "language of the body." This "language" has an important interpersonal meaning, especially in reciprocal relationships between man and woman. Moreover, our previous analyses show that in

this case the "language of the body" should express, at a determinate level, the truth of the sacrament. Participating in the eternal plan of love ("Sacrament hidden in God"), the "language of the body" becomes, in fact, a kind of "prophetism of the body."

It may be said that the Encyclical *Humanae vitae* carries to the extreme consequences—not merely logical and moral, but also practical and pastoral—this truth concerning the human body in its masculinity and femininity.

SACRAMENTAL AND PERSONAL DIMENSION

3. The unity of the two aspects of the problem—of the sacramental (or theological) dimension and of the personalistic one—corresponds to the overall "revelation of the body." From this derives also the connection of the strictly theological vision with the ethical one, which appeals to the "natural law."

The subject of the natural law is, indeed, man not only in the "natural" aspect of his existence, but also in the integral truth of his personal subjectivity. He is shown to us, in revelation, as male and female, in his full temporal and eschatological vocation. He is called by God to be a witness and interpreter of the eternal plan of love, by becoming the minister of the sacrament which "from the beginning" was constituted by the sign of the "union of flesh."

4. As ministers of a sacrament which is constituted by consent and perfected by conjugal union, man and woman are called to express that mysterious "language" of their bodies in all the truth which is proper to it. By means of gestures and reactions, by means of the whole dynamism, reciprocally conditioned, of tension and enjoyment—whose direct source is the body in its masculinity and its femininity, the body in its action and interaction—by means of all this, man, the person, "speaks."

Man and woman carry on in the "language of the body" that dialogue which, according to Genesis 2:24, 25, had its beginning on the day of creation. Precisely on the level of this "language of the body"—which is something more than mere sexual reaction and which, as authentic language of the persons, is subject to the demands of truth, that is, to objective moral norms—man and woman reciprocally express themselves in the fullest and most profound way possible to them by the very corporeal dimension of masculinity and femininity: man and woman express themselves in the measure of the whole truth of the human person.

5. Man is precisely a person because he is master of himself and has self-control. Indeed,

insofar as he is master of himself he can "give himself" to the other. And it is this dimension—the dimension of the liberty of the gift—which becomes essential and decisive for that "language of the body," in which man and woman reciprocally express themselves in the conjugal union. Granted that this is communion of persons, the "language of the body" should be judged according to the criterion of truth. It is precisely this criterion which the Encyclical *Humanae vitae* recalls, as is confirmed by the passages quoted previously.

6. According to the criterion of this truth, which should be expressed in the "language of the body," the conjugal act "signifies" not only love, but also potential fecundity, and therefore it cannot be deprived of its full and adequate significance by artificial means. In the conjugal act it is not licit to separate the unitive aspect from the procreative aspect, because both the one and the other pertain to the intimate truth of the conjugal act: the one is activated together with the other and in a certain sense the one by means of the other. This is what the encyclical teaches (cf. HV 12). Therefore, in such a case the conjugal act deprived of its interior truth, because artificially deprived of its procreative capacity, ceases also to be an act of love.

7. It can be said that in the case of an artificial separation of these two aspects, there is

carried out in the conjugal act a real bodily union, but it does not correspond to the interior truth and to the dignity of personal communion: communion of persons. This communion demands in fact that the "language of the body" be expressed reciprocally in the integral truth of its meaning. If this truth be lacking, one cannot speak either of the truth of self-mastery, or of the truth of the reciprocal gift and of the reciprocal acceptance of self on the part of the person. Such a violation of the interior order of conjugal union, which is rooted in the very order of the person, constitutes the essential evil of the contraceptive act.

REFLECTIONS ON "SIGN"

8. The above-given interpretation of moral doctrine expressed in the Encyclical *Humanae vitae* is situated against the vast background of reflections connected with the theology of the body. Of special validity for this interpretation are the reflections on "sign" in connection with marriage understood as a sacrament. And the essence of the violation which upsets the interior order of the conjugal act cannot be understood in a theologically adequate way, without the reflections on the theme of the "concupiscence of the flesh."

A Discipline that Ennobles Human Love

General audience of August 28, 1984.

1. The Encyclical *Humanae vitae*, while demonstrating the moral evil of contraception, at the same time fully approves of the natural regulation of fertility and, in this sense, it approves of responsible parenthood. Here one must exclude the possibility of describing as "responsible" from the ethical point of view that procreation in which recourse is had to contraception in order to regulate fertility. The true concept of "responsible parenthood" is, on the contrary, connected with the right and lawful regulation of fertility from the ethical viewpoint.

RECOGNIZING VALUES

2. We read in this regard: "The right and lawful ordering of the births of children presup-

poses in husband and wife first and foremost that they fully recognize and value the true blessings of family life, and secondly, that they acquire complete mastery over themselves and their emotions. For if with the aid of reason and of free will they are to control their natural drives, there can be no doubt at all of the need for self-denial. Only then will the expression of love, particular to married life, conform to right order. And this is especially true as regards the practice of periodic continence. But self-discipline of this kind is a shining witness to the chastity of husband and wife and, so far from being a hindrance to their love of one another, transforms it by giving it a more truly human character. And if this self-discipline does demand that they persevere in their purpose and efforts, it has at the same time the salutary effect of enabling husband and wife to develop to the full their personalities and be enriched with spiritual blessings..." (HV 21).

THE PROPER ATTITUDE

3. The encyclical then points out the consequences of such a line of conduct not merely for the couple themselves but also for the whole family understood as a community of persons. It will be necessary to treat again of this subject. The encyclical underlines that a right and lawful

regulation of fertility demands above all from husband and wife a definite family and procreative attitude: that is to say, it requires "that they acquire and possess solid convictions about the true values of life and of the family" (HV 21). Beginning from this premise, it was necessary to proceed to an overall consideration of the question as was done by the Synod of Bishops of 1980 ("On the Role of the Christian Family"). Later, the doctrine concerning this particular problem of conjugal and family morality, treated in the Encyclical *Humanae vitae,* found its proper place and fitting perspective in the comprehensive context of the Apostolic Exhortation *Familiaris consortio.* The theology of the body, particularly as the pedagogy of the body, has its roots, in a certain sense, in the theology of the family and, at the same time, leads to it. This pedagogy of the body, whose key today is the Encyclical *Humanae vitae,* is explained only in the full context of a correct vision of the values of life and of the family.

4. In the text quoted above Pope Paul VI refers to conjugal chastity when he writes that the observance of periodic continence is the form of self-mastery in which "conjugal chastity" is manifested (HV 21).

In undertaking now a deeper analysis of this problem it is necessary to bear in mind the whole doctrine on chastity understood as the life of the Spirit (cf. Gal. 5:25), already considered by us previously, in order to understand the respective statements of the encyclical on the theme of "periodic continence." That doctrine remains indeed the real reason, beginning from which the teaching of Paul VI defines the regulation of births and responsible parenthood as ethically right and lawful.

Even though the "periodicity" of continence is in this case applied to the so-called "natural rhythms" (HV 16), however, the continence itself is a definite and permanent moral attitude; it is a *virtue,* and therefore, the whole line of conduct guided by it acquires a virtuous character. The encyclical emphasizes clearly enough that here it is not merely a matter of a definite "technique," but of *ethics* in the strict sense of the term as the *morality of conduct.*

Therefore, the encyclical opportunely sets out in relief, on the one hand, the necessity to respect in the above-mentioned line of conduct the order established by the Creator, and on the other hand, the necessity of an immediate motivation of an ethical character.

5. In regard to the first aspect we read: "To experience the gift of married love while respecting the laws of conception is to acknowledge that one is not the master of the sources of life, but rather the minister of the design established by the Creator" (HV 13). "Human life is

sacred"—as our Predecessor of holy memory, John XXIII, said in his Encyclical *Mater et magistra*—"from its very beginning it involves directly the creative action of God" (*AAS* 53, 1961; cf. HV 13). As regards the immediate motivation, the Encyclical *Humanae vitae* requires that "there exist reasonable grounds for spacing births, arising from the physical or psychological condition of husband or wife, or from external circumstances..." (HV 16).

LIVING BY THE SPIRIT

6. In the case of a morally upright regulation of fertility effected by means of periodic continence, one is clearly dealing with the practice of conjugal chastity, that is, of a definite ethical attitude. In biblical language we could say that it is a case of living by the Spirit (cf. Gal. 5:25).

The morally correct regulation is also called "the *natural* regulation of fertility," which can be explained as conformity to the "natural law." By "natural law" we mean that "order of nature" in the field of procreation, insofar as it is understood by right reason: this order is the expression of the Creator's plan for man. And it is precisely this that the encyclical, together with the whole Tradition of Christian teaching and practice, stresses in a particular way: the virtuous character of the attitude which is expressed in the "natural" regulation of fertility is determined not so much by fidelity to an impersonal "natural law" as to the Creator-Person, the Source and Lord of the order which is manifested in such a law.

From this point of view, the reduction to a mere biological regularity, separated from the "order of nature" that is, from the "Creator's plan," deforms the authentic thought of the Encyclical *Humanae vitae* (cf. HV 14).

The document certainly presupposes that biological regularity—indeed, it exhorts competent persons to study it and to apply it in a still deeper way—but it always understands this regularity as the expression of the "order of nature," that is, of the providential plan of the Creator, in the faithful execution of which the true good of the human person consists.

Responsible Parenthood Linked to Moral Maturity

General audience of September 5, 1984.

"The Lord was witness to the covenant between you and the wife of your youth.... Has not the one God made and sustained for us the spirit of life? What does he desire? Godly offspring. So take heed to yourselves and let none be faithless to the wife of his youth" (Mal. 2:14-15).

1. We have previously spoken of the right and lawful regulation of fertility according to the doctrine contained in the Encyclical *Humanae vitae* (HV 19), and in the Exhortation *Familiaris consortio*. The description of "natural," attributed to the morally correct regulation of fertility (following the natural rhythms, cf. HV 16), is explained by the fact that that manner of conduct corresponds to the truth of the person and therefore to his dignity: a dignity which by

"nature" belongs to man as a rational and free being. Man, as a rational free being, can and must reread with discernment that biological rhythm which belongs to the natural order. He can and must conform to it so as to exercise that "responsible parenthood," which, according to the Creator's design, is inscribed in the natural order of human fecundity. The concept of a morally correct regulation of fertility is nothing other than the rereading of the "language of the body" in truth. The very "natural rhythms immanent in the generative functions" pertain to the objective truth of that language, which the persons concerned should reread in its full objective content. It is necessary to bear in mind that the "body speaks" not merely with the whole external expression of masculinity and femininity, but also with the internal structures of the organism, of the somatic and psycho-somatic reaction. All this should find its appropriate place in that language in which husband and wife dialogue with each other, as persons called to the communion of the "union of the body."

AT THE COST
OF A PRECISE SELF-DENIAL

2. All efforts directed to an ever more precise knowledge of those "natural rhythms" which are manifested in relation to human

procreation, all efforts of family counselors and indeed of the couple themselves, are not aimed at making the language of the body merely "biological" (at "reducing ethics to biology," as some have mistakenly held), but exclusively at ensuring the integral truth of that "language of the body" in which husband and wife should express themselves in a mature way before the demands of responsible parenthood.

The Encyclical *Humanae vitae* stresses several times that "responsible parenthood" is connected with a continual effort and commitment, and that it is put into effect at the cost of a precise self-denial (cf. HV 21). All these and other similar expressions show that in the case of "responsible parenthood," or of a morally correct regulation of fertility, it is a question of *the real good of human persons and of what corresponds to the true dignity of the person.*

RIGHT CONSCIENCE IS THE TRUE INTERPRETER

3. The use of the "infertile periods" for conjugal union can be an abuse if the couple, for unworthy reasons, seeks in this way to avoid having children, thus lowering the number of births in their family below the morally correct level. This morally correct level must be estab-

lished by taking into account not only the good of one's own family, and even the state of health and the means of the couple themselves, but also the good of the society to which they belong, of the Church, and even of the whole of mankind.

The Encyclical *Humanae vitae* presents "responsible parenthood" as an expression of a high ethical value. In no way is it exclusively directed to limiting, much less excluding, children; it means also the willingness to accept a larger family. Above all, according to the Encyclical *Humanae vitae*, "responsible parenthood" implies "a deeper relationship with the objective moral order instituted by God—the order of which a right conscience is the true interpreter" (HV 10).

MORAL MATURITY

4. The truth of "responsible parenthood" and its implementation is linked with the moral maturity of the person, and it is here that there is very frequently revealed the divergence between what the encyclical explicitly regards as of primary importance and the general viewpoint on the subject.

The encyclical places in relief the ethical dimension of the problem, by underlining the role of the virtue of temperance correctly understood. Within the scope of this dimension there is also an adequate "method" for acting. In the common viewpoint it frequently happens that the "method," separated from the ethical dimension proper to it, is put into effect in a merely functional, and even utilitarian, way. By separating the "natural method" from the ethical dimension, one no longer sees the difference between it and the other "methods" (artificial means) and one comes to the point of speaking of it as if it were only a different form of contraception.

5. From the point of view of the true doctrine expressed by the Encyclical *Humanae vitae,* it is therefore important to present this method correctly, and reference is made to this in the same document (cf. HV 16). Above all it is important to examine in depth the ethical dimension, for it is in reference to this that the method, as "natural," acquires its significance as a "morally correct," upright method. And therefore within the framework of the present analysis, it is fitting that we should turn our attention principally to what the encyclical states on the subject of self-mastery and on *continence.* Without a searching interpretation of that subject we shall not arrive either at the heart of the moral truth, or at the heart of the anthropological truth

of the problem. Beforehand it was already pointed out that the roots of this problem lie deep in the theology of the body: it is this (when it becomes, as it ought to, the pedagogy of the body) which constitutes in reality the morally right and lawful "method" of the regulation of births, understood in its deepest and fullest sense.

LAWFUL REGULATION

6. Later when describing the specifically moral values of the "natural" regulation of fertility (that is, lawful or morally right), the author of *Humanae vitae* writes as follows: "This self-discipline...brings to family life abundant fruits of tranquillity and peace. It helps in solving difficulties of other kinds. It fosters in husband and wife thoughtfulness and loving consideration for each other. It helps them to repel the excessive self-love which is the opposite of charity. It arouses in them a consciousness of their responsibilities. And finally, it confers upon parents a deeper and more effective influence in the education of their children. For these latter, both in childhood and in youth, as years go by, develop a right sense of values as regards the true blessings of life and achieve a serene and harmonious use of their mental and physical powers" (HV 21).

7. The passage cited completes the picture of what the Encyclical *Humanae vitae* means by "the right and lawful ordering of the births of children" (HV 21). This is, as can be seen, not merely "a mode of behavior" in a specific field, but an attitude which is based on the integral moral maturity of the persons and at the same time completes it.

Prayer, Penance and the Eucharist Are the Principal Sources of Spirituality for Married Couples

General audience of October 3, 1984.

1. Referring to the doctrine contained in the Encyclical *Humanae vitae*, we will try to further outline the spiritual life of married couples.

Here are the great words of this encyclical: "While the Church does indeed hand on to her children the inviolable conditions laid down by God's law, she is also the herald of salvation and through the sacraments she flings wide open the channels of grace through which man is made a new creature responding in charity and true freedom to the design of his Creator and Savior, experiencing too the sweetness of the yoke of Christ.

"In humble obedience then to her voice, let Christian husbands and wives be mindful of their vocation to the Christian life, a vocation which, deriving from their Baptism, has been confirmed anew and made more explicit by the Sacrament of Matrimony. For by this sacrament they are strengthened and, one might also say, consecrated to the faithful fulfillment of their duties; to realizing to the full their vocation; and to bearing witness, as becomes them, to Christ before the world. For the Lord has entrusted to them the task of making visible to men and women the holiness, and the joy too, of the law which unites inseparably their love for one another and the cooperation they give to God's love, God who is the Author of human life" (HV 25).

MORALLY EVIL ACT

2. By showing the moral evil of the contraceptive act and by outlining at the same time a possibly integral framework for the "honest" practice of fertility regulation, that is, of responsible fatherhood and motherhood, the Encyclical *Humanae vitae* creates the premises that allow us to draw the great lines of the Christian

spirituality of the conjugal vocation and life, and likewise the spirituality of parents and of the family.

It can further be said that the encyclical presupposes the entire tradition of this spirituality, which is rooted in biblical sources, already previously analyzed, by offering the opportunity to reflect on them anew and to build an adequate synthesis.

It is well to recall here what was said about the organic relationship between the theology of the body and the pedagogy of the body. This "theology-pedagogy," in fact, already constitutes *per se* the essential nucleus of conjugal spirituality. And this is indicated also by the above-quoted sentences from the encyclical.

INTEGRAL INTENTION

3. Anyone would certainly read and interpret the Encyclical *Humanae vitae* erroneously who would see in it only the reduction of "responsible fatherhood and motherhood" to mere "biological rhythm of fertility." The author of the encyclical energetically disapproves of and contradicts any form of reductive interpretation (and in such a "partial" sense), and insistently reproposes the integral intention. Responsible fatherhood and motherhood, under-

stood integrally, is none other than an important element of all conjugal and family spirituality, that is, of that vocation about which the cited text of *Humanae vitae* speaks when it states that the married couple must "realize to the full their vocation" (HV 25). It is the Sacrament of Marriage that strengthens them and, one would say, consecrates them to its fulfillment (cf. HV 25).

In the light of the doctrine expressed in the encyclical, it is well to become more aware of that "strengthening power" that is united to the *"sui generis* consecration" of the Sacrament of Marriage.

Since the analysis of the ethical problem of Paul VI's document was centered above all on the exactness of the *respective norm,* the sketch of conjugal spirituality which is found there intends to place in relief precisely those "powers" which make possible the authentic Christian witness of married life.

DIFFICULTIES PRESENT

4. "We have no wish at all to pass over in silence the difficulties, at times very great, which beset the lives of Christian married couples. For them, as indeed for every one of us, 'the gate is narrow and the way is hard that leads to life' (cf. Mt. 7:14). Nevertheless, it is precisely the hope of that life which, like a brightly

burning torch, lights up their journey, as, strong in spirit, they strive to live 'sober, upright, and godly lives in this world' (cf. Ti. 2:12) knowing for sure that 'the form of this world is passing away' (cf. 1 Cor. 7:31)" (HV 25).

In the encyclical, the view of married life is at every step marked by Christian realism, and it is precisely this which helps more greatly to acquire those "powers" which allow the formation of the spirituality of married couples and parents in the spirit of an authentic pedagogy of heart and body.

The very awareness "of that future life" opens up, so to speak, a broad horizon of those powers that must guide them through the hard way (cf. HV 25) and lead them through the narrow gate (cf. HV 25) of their evangelical vocation.

The encyclical says: "For this reason husbands and wives should take up the burden appointed to them, willingly, in the strength of faith and of that hope which 'does not disappoint us, because God's love has been poured out into our hearts through the Holy Spirit who has been given to us' (Rom. 5:5)" (HV 25).

BY THE HOLY SPIRIT

5. Here is the essential and fundamental "power": *the love planted in the heart* ("poured

out into our hearts") *by the Holy Spirit*. Consequently, the encyclical points out how the married couple must implore this essential "power" and every other "divine help" by prayer; how they must draw grace and love from the ever-living fountain of the Eucharist; how they must overcome "with humble perseverance" their deficiencies and sins in the Sacrament of Penance.

These are the means—*infallible and indispensable*—for forming the Christian spirituality of married life and family life. With these, that essential and spiritual creative "power" of love reaches human hearts and, at the same time, human bodies in their subjective masculinity and femininity. This love, in fact, allows the building of the whole life of the married couple according to that "truth of the sign," by means of which marriage is built up in its sacramental dignity, as the central point of the encyclical reveals (cf. HV 12).

The Power of Love Is Given to Man and Woman as a Share in God's Love

General audience of October 10, 1984.

1. We are continuing to outline the spirituality of married life in the light of the Encyclical *Humanae vitae*.

According to the doctrine contained there, in conformity with biblical sources and all Tradition, *love*, from the subjective viewpoint, is a *power*, that is, a capacity of the human soul, of a theological nature. It is therefore the power given to man in order to participate in that love with which God Himself loves in the mystery of creation and redemption. It is that love which "rejoices with the truth" (1 Cor. 13:6), that is, in which there is expressed the spiritual joy (Augustine's "enjoyment") of every authentic value: a joy like that of the Creator Himself, who in the beginning saw that everything "was very good" (Gn. 1:31).

If the powers of concupiscence try to detach the "language of the body" from the truth, that is, they try to falsify it, the power of love instead strengthens it ever anew in that truth, so that the mystery of the redemption of the body can bear fruit in it.

THE FULLNESS OF GOOD

2. Love itself—which makes possible and brings about conjugal dialogue according to the full truth of the life of the spouses—is at the same time a power or a capacity of a moral nature, actively oriented toward the fullness of good and for this very reason toward every true good. And therefore its role consists in safeguarding the inseparable connection between the "two meanings of the conjugal act," with which the encyclical deals (HV 12), that is to say, in protecting both the value of the true union of the couple (that is, the personal communion) and the value of responsible fatherhood and motherhood (in the form that is mature and worthy of man).

LOVE COORDINATES

3. According to traditional language, love, as a higher power, coordinates the actions of the persons, the husband and the wife, in the sphere of the purposes of marriage. Although neither the conciliar constitution nor the encyclical, in dealing with the question, use the language at one time customary, they nonetheless deal with what the traditional expressions refer to.

Love, as a higher power that the man and the woman receive from God along with the particular "consecration" of the Sacrament of Marriage, involves a correct coordination of the purposes, according to which—in the traditional teaching of the Church—there is constituted the moral (or rather "theological and moral") order of the life of the couple.

The doctrine of the Constitution *Gaudium et spes,* as well as that of the Encyclical *Humanae vitae,* clarifies the same moral order in reference to love, understood as a higher power that confers adequate content and value to conjugal acts according to the truth of the two meanings, the unitive and the procreative, with respect for their inseparability.

In this renewed formulation the traditional teaching on the purposes of marriage (and their hierarchy) is reaffirmed and at the same time deepened from the viewpoint of the interior life of the spouses, that is, of conjugal and family spirituality.

4. The role of love, which is "poured out into [the] hearts" (Rom. 5:5) of the spouses as the fundamental spiritual power of their conjugal pact, consists—as was said—in protecting both the value of the true communion of the spouses and the value of truly responsible fatherhood and motherhood. The power of love—authentic in the theological and ethical sense—is expressed in this, that love *correctly unites "the two meanings of the conjugal act,"* excluding not only in theory but above all in practice the "contradiction" that might be evidenced in this field. This "contradiction" is the most frequent reason for objecting to the Encyclical *Humanae vitae* and the teaching of the Church. There must be a well-examined analysis, and not only theological but also anthropological (we have tried to do this in the whole present reflection), to show that there is no need here to speak of "contradiction," but only of "difficulty." Well then, the encyclical itself stresses this "difficulty" in various passages.

And this arises from the fact that the power of love is implanted in man lured by concupiscence: in human subjects love does battle with threefold concupiscence (cf. 1 Jn. 2:16), in particular with the concupiscence of the flesh which distorts the truth of the "language of the body." And therefore love too is not able to be realized in the truth of the "language of the body" except through overcoming concupiscence.

LINKED WITH CHASTITY

5. If the key element of the spirituality of spouses and parents—that essential "power" which spouses must continually draw from the sacramental "consecration"—is *love*, this love, as it is seen from the text of the encyclical (HV 20), is by its nature linked with the chastity that is manifested as mastery over oneself, that is, continence: in particular, as periodic continence. In biblical language, the author of the letter to the Ephesians seems to allude to this when in his "classic" text he exhorts spouses to "defer to one another out of reverence for Christ" (Eph. 5:21).

We can say that the Encyclical *Humanae vitae* constitutes precisely the development of this biblical truth about conjugal and family Christian spirituality. Nonetheless, to make it more manifest, there needs to be a deeper analysis of the virtue of continence and of its special significance for the truth of the mutual "language of the body" in married life and (indirectly) in the whole sphere of mutual relationships between man and woman.

Continence Protects the Dignity of the Conjugal Act

General audience of October 24, 1984.

1. In keeping with what has already been said, today we will take up the analysis of the virtue of continence.

Continence, which is part of the more general virtue of temperance, consists in the capacity to dominate, control and direct drives of a sexual character (concupiscence of the flesh) and their consequences, in the psychosomatic subjectivity of man. This capacity, insofar as it is a constant disposition of the will, merits being called a virtue.

We know from the previous analyses that concupiscence of the flesh, and the corresponding "desire" of a sexual character aroused by it, is expressed with a specific impulse in the sphere of somatic reaction and also with a psycho-emotive excitement of the sensual impulse.

The personal subject, in order to succeed in mastering this impulse and excitement, must be committed to a progressive education in self-control of the will, of the feelings, of the emotions; and this education must develop beginning with the most simple acts in which it is relatively easy to put the interior decision into practice. This presupposes, as is obvious, the clear perception of the values expressed in the law and the consequent formation of firm convictions which, if accompanied by the respective disposition of the will, give rise to the corresponding virtue. This is precisely the virtue of continence (self-mastery), which is seen to be the fundamental condition for the reciprocal language of the body to remain in the truth and for the couple to "defer to one another out of reverence for Christ," according to the words in Scripture (Eph. 5:21). This "deferring to one another" means the common concern for the truth of the "language of the body"; rather, deferring "out of reverence for Christ" indicates the gift of the fear of God (a gift of the Holy Spirit) which accompanies the virtue of continence.

2. This is very important for an adequate understanding of the virtue of continence and especially of the so-called "periodic continence" dealt with in the Encyclical *Humanae vitae*. The conviction that the virtue of continence "is set

against" the concupiscence of the flesh is correct, but it is not altogether complete. It is not complete especially when we take into account the fact that this virtue does not appear and does not act abstractly and therefore in isolation, but always in connection with the other virtues (*nexus virtutum*), therefore in connection with prudence, justice, fortitude and above all with charity.

In the light of these considerations it is easy to understand that continence is not limited to offering resistance to the concupiscence of the flesh; but through this resistance it is open likewise to those values, more profound and more mature, inherent in the spousal signifi-cance of the body in its femininity and masculin-ity, as well as in the authentic freedom of the gift in the reciprocal relations of the persons. Concupiscence of the flesh itself, insofar as it seeks above all carnal and sensual satisfaction, makes man in a certain sense blind and insensi-tive to the most profound values that spring from love and which at the same time constitute love in the interior truth that is proper to it.

LINKED TO THE POWER OF LOVE

3. In this way there is manifested also the essential character of conjugal chastity in its organic link with the "power" of love, which is

poured out into the hearts of the married couple along with the "consecration" of the Sacrament of Marriage. In addition, it becomes evident that the call directed to the couple that they "defer to one another out of reverence for Christ" (Eph. 5:21) seems to open that interior space in which both become ever more sensitive to the most profound and most mature values that are connected with the spousal significance of the body and with the true freedom of the gift.

If conjugal chastity (and chastity in general) is manifested at first as the capacity to resist the concupiscence of the flesh, it later gradually reveals itself as a singular capacity to perceive, love and practice those meanings of the "language of the body" which remain altogether unknown to concupiscence itself and which progressively enrich the marital dialogue of the couple, purifying it, deepening it, and at the same time simplifying it.

Therefore, that asceticism of continence, of which the encyclical speaks (HV 21), does not impoverish "affective manifestations," but rather makes them spiritually more intense and therefore enriches them.

NO CONTRADICTION

4. Analyzing continence in this way, in the dynamics proper to this virtue (anthropological, ethical and theological), we see that that appar-

ent "contradiction" disappears which is often an objection to the Encyclical *Humanae vitae* and to the doctrine of the Church on conjugal morality. That is, there would be a "contradiction" (according to those who offer this objection) between the two meanings of the conjugal act, the unitive meaning and the procreative meaning (cf. HV 12), so that if it were not licit to separate them, the couple would be deprived of the right to conjugal union when they could not responsibly be permitted to procreate.

The Encyclical *Humanae vitae* gives an answer to this apparent contradiction, if one studies it in depth. In fact, Pope Paul VI confirms that there is no "contradiction" but only a "difficulty" connected with the whole interior situation of the "man of concupiscence." Rather, precisely by reason of this "difficulty" there is assigned to the interior and ascetical commitment of the couple the true order of conjugal life, in view of which they become "strengthened and, one might say, consecrated" (HV 25) by the Sacrament of Marriage.

ADEQUATE MEANING

5. That order of conjugal life means in addition the subjective harmony between parenthood (responsible) and personal communion, a harmony created by conjugal chastity. In it, in

fact, there mature the interior fruits of continence. Through this interior maturing, the conjugal act itself acquires the importance and dignity proper to it in its potentially procreative meaning. At the same time, all the "affective manifestations" acquire an adequate meaning (HV 21), and they serve to express the personal communion of the couple in proportion to the subjective richness of femininity and masculinity.

PARTICULAR AFFECTION

6. In keeping with experience and tradition, the encyclical reveals that the conjugal act is also a "manifestation of affection" (HV 16), but a "manifestation of particular affection" because at the same time it has a potentially procreative meaning. As a result, it is oriented to express personal union, but not only that. At the same time the encyclical, although indirectly, indicates many "manifestations of affection," effective exclusively to express the personal union of the couple.

The role of conjugal chastity, and still more precisely that of continence, lies not only in protecting the importance and dignity of the conjugal act in relation to its procreative meaning, but also in safeguarding the importance and the dignity proper to the conjugal act as expressive of interpersonal union, revealing to the awareness and the experience of the couple all the other possible "manifestations of affection" that can express this profound communion of theirs.

It is indeed a matter of not doing harm to the communion of the couple in the case where for just reasons they should abstain from the conjugal act. And still more, that this communion—continually being built up, day by day, through suitable "affective manifestations"—may constitute, so to speak, a vast terrain on which, under suitable conditions, the decision for a morally right conjugal act matures.

Continence Frees One from Inner Tension

General audience of October 31, 1984.

1. We are continuing the analysis of continence in the light of the teaching contained in *Humanae vitae*.

It is often thought that continence causes inner tensions from which man must free himself. In the light of the analyses we have done, continence, understood integrally, is rather the only *way to free man from such tensions*. It means nothing other than the spiritual effort aimed at expressing the "language of the body," not only in truth but also in the authentic richness of the "manifestations of affection."

ESSENTIAL REASONS

2. Is this effort possible? In other words (and under another aspect) there returns here the question about the "feasibility of the moral

law" recalled and confirmed by *Humanae vitae*. It constitutes one of the most essential questions (and currently also one of the most urgent ones) in the sphere of the spirituality of marriage.

The Church is totally convinced of the correctness of the principle that affirms responsible fatherhood and motherhood—in the sense explained in previous catecheses—and this not only for "demographic" reasons but for more essential reasons. *We call that fatherhood and that motherhood responsible which correspond to the personal dignity of the couple* as parents, to the *truth* of their person and of the conjugal *act*. Hence arises the close and direct relationship that links this dimension with the whole spirituality of marriage.

Pope Paul VI, in *Humanae vitae,* expressed what elsewhere had been affirmed by many authoritative moralists and scientists, even non-Catholics[1]—namely, that precisely in this field, so profoundly and essentially human and personal, it is necessary above all to refer to man as a person, the subject who decides by himself, and not to "means" which make him the "object" (of manipulations) and "depersonalize" him. It is therefore a question here of an authentically "humanistic" meaning of the development and progress of human civilization.

PERSONAL DIMENSION

3. Is this effort possible? The whole question of the Encyclical *Humanae vitae* is not reduced simply to the biological dimension of human fertility (the question of the "natural cycles of fertility"), but goes back to the very subjectivity of man, to that personal "I" through which the person is man or woman.

Already during the discussion in the Second Vatican Council, in relation to the chapter of *Gaudium et spes* on the "Dignity of Marriage and the Family and its Promotion," there was discussed the necessity for a deepened analysis of the reactions (and also of the emotions) connected with the mutual influence of masculinity and femininity on the human subject.[2] This question belongs not so much to biology as to psychology: from biology and psychology it then passes into the sphere of the spirituality of marriage and the family. Here, in fact, this question is in close relationship with the way of understanding the virtue of continence, that is, self-mastery and, in particular, of periodic continence.

UNDERSTANDING CONTINENCE

4. A careful analysis of human psychology (which is at the same time a subjective self-analysis and then becomes an analysis of an

"object" accessible to human knowledge) allows us to arrive at some other essential affirmations. In fact, in interpersonal relationships in which the mutual influence of masculinity and femininity is expressed, there is freed in the psycho-emotive subject in the human "I," alongside a reaction distinguishable as "excitement," another reaction that can and must be called "emotion." Although these two kinds of reaction appear joined, it is possible to distinguish them experimentally and to "differentiate them" with regard to their content or their "object."[3]

The objective difference between the one and the other kind of reaction consists in the fact that the excitement is above all "corporeal" and in this sense "sensual"; emotion, on the other hand—even though aroused by the mutual reaction of masculinity and femininity—refers above all to the other person understood in the person's "integrality." We can say that this is an "emotion caused by the person," in relation to the person's masculinity or femininity.

5. What we are stating here with regard to the psychology of the mutual reactions of masculinity and femininity helps in understanding the role of the virtue of continence, about which we spoke previously. Continence is not only—and not even principally—the ability to "abstain," that is, mastery over the multiple reactions that

are interwoven in the mutual influence of masculinity and femininity: such a role would be defined as "negative." But there is also another role (which we can call "positive") of self-mastery: it is the ability to direct the respective reactions, both as to their content and their character.

It has already been said that in the field of the mutual reactions of masculinity and femininity "excitement" and "emotion" appear not only as two distinct and different experiences of the human "I," but very often they appear joined in the sphere of the same experience as two different elements of that experience. The reciprocal degree to which these two elements appear in a given experience depends on various circumstances of an interior and an exterior nature. At times one of the elements is clearly prevalent; at other times there is rather a balance between them.

MAINTAINING THE BALANCE

6. As the ability to direct "excitement" and "emotion" in the sphere of the mutual influence of masculinity and femininity, continence has the essential task of maintaining the balance between the communion in which the couple wish to mutually express only their intimate union and that in which (at least implicitly) they accept

responsible parenthood. In fact, "excitement" and "emotion" can jeopardize, on the part of the subject, the orientation and the character of the mutual "language of the body."

Excitement seeks above all to be expressed in the form of sensual and corporeal pleasure, that is, it tends toward the conjugal act which (depending on the "natural cycles of fertility") includes the possibility of procreation. *Emotion,* on the other hand, caused by another human being as a person, even if in its emotive content it is conditioned by the femininity or masculinity of the "other," does not *per se* tend toward the conjugal act, but limits itself to other "manifestations of affection," in which there is expressed the spousal meaning of the body, and which nevertheless do not include its (potentially) procreative meaning.

It is easy to understand what conclusions arise from this with respect to the question of responsible fatherhood and motherhood. These conclusions are of a moral nature.

FOOTNOTES

1. Cf., for example, the statements of the *"Bund fur evangelisch-katholische Wiedervereinigung"* (L'O. R., 9-19-1968, p. 3); Dr. F. King, Anglican (L'O. R., 10-5-1968, p. 3); and also the Muslim, Mr. Mohammed Cherif Zeghoudu (in the same issue). Especially significant is the

letter written on November 28, 1968, to Cardinal Cicognani by Karl Barth, in which he praised the great courage of Paul VI.

2. Cf. the interventions by Card. Leo Suenens at the 13th General Congregation on September 29, 1968: *Acta Synodalia S. Concilii Oecumenici Vaticani II,* vol. 4, part 3, p. 30.

3. In this regard we should recall what St. Thomas says in a final analysis of human love in relation to the "concupiscible" and to the will (cf. *Summa Theologiae* I-IIae, q. 26, art. 2).

Continence Deepens
Personal Communion

General audience of November 7, 1984.

1. We are continuing the analysis of the virtue of continence in the light of the doctrine contained in the Encyclical *Humanae vitae*.

It is well to recall that the great classics of ethical (and anthropological) thought, both the pre-Christian ones and the Christian ones (St. Thomas Aquinas), see in the virtue of continence not only the capacity to "contain" bodily and sensual reactions, but even more the capacity to control and guide man's whole sensual and emotive sphere. In the case under discussion, it is a question of the capacity to direct the line of excitement toward its correct development and also the line of emotion itself, orienting it toward the deepening and interior intensification of its "pure" and, in a certain sense, "disinterested" character.

NOT AN OPPOSITION

2. This differentiation between the line of excitement and the line of emotion is not an opposition. It does not mean that the conjugal act, as a result of excitement, does not at the same time involve the deep emotion of the other person. Certainly it does, or at any rate, it should not be otherwise.

In the conjugal act, the intimate union should involve a particular intensification of emotion, or rather the deep emotion, of the other person. This is also contained in the Letter to the Ephesians in the form of an exhortation directed to married couples: "Defer to one another out of reverence for Christ" (Eph. 5:21).

The distinction between "excitement" and "emotion," noted in this analysis, proves only the subjective reactive-emotive richness of the human "I." This richness excludes any unilateral reduction and enables the virtue of continence to be practiced as a capacity to direct the manifesting of both the excitement and the emotion, aroused by the reciprocal reacting of masculinity and femininity.

NATURAL METHOD

3. The virtue of continence, so understood, has an essential role in maintaining the interior balance between the two meanings, the unitive

and the procreative, of the conjugal act (cf. HV 12) in view of a truly responsible fatherhood and motherhood.

The Encyclical *Humanae vitae* devotes due attention to the biological aspect of the question, that is to say, to the rhythmic character of human fertility. Even though this "periodicalness" can be called, in the light of the encyclical, a providential index for a responsible fatherhood and motherhood, nevertheless a question such as this one, which has such a profoundly personalistic and sacramental (theological) meaning, is not resolved only on this level.

The encyclical teaches responsible fatherhood and motherhood "as a proof of a mature conjugal love"—and therefore it contains not only the answer to the concrete question that is asked in the sphere of the ethics of married life but, as already has been stated, it also indicates a plan of conjugal spirituality, which we wish at least to outline.

MAINTAINS BALANCE

4. The correct way of intending and practicing periodic continence as a virtue (that is, according to *Humanae vitae* no. 21, the "mastery of self") also essentially determines the "naturalness" of the method, called also the

"natural method": this is "naturalness" at the
level of the person. Therefore there can be no
thought of a mechanical application of biological
laws. The knowledge itself of the "rhythms of
fertility" — even though indispensable — still
does not create that interior freedom of the gift,
which is by its nature explicitly spiritual and
depends on man's interior maturity. This freedom presupposes such a capacity to direct the
sensual and emotive reactions as to make possible the giving of self to the other "I" on the
grounds of the mature self-possession of
one's own "I" in its corporeal and emotive
subjectivity.

COMMUNION OF PERSONS

5. As we know from the biblical and theological analyses we have previously done, the
human body in its masculinity and femininity is
interiorly ordered to the communion of the
persons *(communio personarum)*. Its spousal
meaning consists in this.

The very spousal meaning of the body has
been distorted, almost at its very roots, by
concupiscence (particularly by the concupiscence of the flesh in the sphere of the "threefold
concupiscence"). The virtue of continence in its
mature form gradually reveals the "pure" aspect

of the spousal meaning of the body. In this way, continence develops the personal communion of the man and the woman, a communion that cannot be formed and developed in the full truth of its possibilities only on the level of concupiscence. This is precisely what the Encyclical *Humanae vitae* affirms. This truth has two aspects: the personalistic and the theological.

Respect for the Work of God

General audience of November 21, 1984.

1. On the basis of the doctrine contained in the Encyclical *Humanae vitae,* we intend to trace an outline of conjugal spirituality. In the spiritual life of married couples there are at work the gifts of the Holy Spirit, especially the "gift of piety," that is, the gift of respect for what is a work of God.

2. This gift, together with love and chastity, helps to identify, in the sum total of married life, that act in which, at least potentially, the spousal meaning of the body is linked with the procreative meaning. It leads to understanding, among the possible "manifestations of affection," the singular, or rather the exceptional, significance of that act: its dignity and the consequent

serious responsibility connected with it. Therefore, the antithesis of conjugal spirituality is constituted, in a certain sense, by the subjective lack of this understanding which is linked to contraceptive practice and mentality. In addition to everything else, this does an enormous harm from the point of view of man's interior culture. The virtue of conjugal chastity, and still more the gift of respect for what comes from God, mold the couple's spirituality to the purpose of protecting the particular dignity of this act, of this "manifestation of affection" in which the truth of the "language of the body" can be expressed only by safeguarding the procreative potential.

Responsible fatherhood and motherhood means the spiritual appraisal—conforming to truth—of the conjugal act in the knowledge and in the will of both spouses, who in this "manifestation of affection," after considering the interior and external circumstances, especially the biological ones, express their mature readiness for fatherhood and motherhood.

3. Respect for the work of God contributes to seeing that the conjugal act does not become diminished and deprived of the interior meaning of married life as a whole—that it does not become a "habit"—and that there is expressed in it a sufficient fullness of personal and ethical content, and also of religious content, that is, veneration for the majesty of the Creator, the

only and the ultimate depositary of the source of life, and for the spousal love of the Redeemer. All this creates and enlarges, so to speak, the interior space for the mutual freedom of the gift in which there is fully manifested the spousal meaning of masculinity and femininity.

The obstacle to this freedom is presented by the interior constriction of concupiscence, directed to the other "I" as an object of pleasure. Respect for what is created by God gives freedom from this constriction; it frees from all that reduces the other "I" to a mere object: it strengthens the interior freedom of the gift.

4. This can happen only through a profound appreciation of the personal dignity of both the feminine "I" and the masculine "I" in their shared life. This spiritual appreciation is the fundamental fruit of the gift of the Spirit which urges the person to respect the work of God. From this appreciation, and therefore indirectly from that gift, all the "affectionate manifestations" which make up the fabric of remaining faithful to the union of marriage derive their true spousal meaning. This union is expressed through the conjugal act only in given circumstances, but it can and it must be manifested continually, every day, through various "affectionate manifestations" which are determined by the capacity of a "disinterested" emotion of the "I" in relation to femininity and, reciprocally, in relation to masculinity.

The attitude of respect for the work of God, which the Spirit stirs up in the couple, has an enormous significance for those "affectionate manifestations," since side by side with it there is the capacity for deep satisfaction, admiration, disinterested attention to the "visible" and at the same time the "invisible" beauty of femininity and masculinity, and finally a deep appreciation for the disinterested gift of the "other."

5. All this determines the spiritual identification of what is male or female, of what is "corporeal" and at the same time personal. From this spiritual identification there emerges the awareness of the union "through the body," in safeguarding the interior freedom of the gift. Through the "affectionate manifestations" the couple help each other remain faithful to the union; and at the same time these "manifestations" protect in each of them that "deep-rooted peace" which is in a certain sense the interior resonance of chastity guided by the gift of respect for what is created by God.

This gift involves a profound and universal attention to the person in one's masculinity and femininity, thus creating the interior climate suitable for personal communion. Only in this climate of the personal communion of the couple does there rightly mature that procreation which we describe as "responsible."

6. The Encyclical *Humanae vitae* enables us to trace an outline of conjugal spirituality.

This is the human and supernatural climate in which—taking the "biological" order into consideration and, at the same time, on the basis of chastity sustained by the "gift of piety"—is formed the interior harmony of marriage, in respect for what the encyclical calls "the twofold significance of the conjugal act" (HV 12). This harmony means that the couple live together in the interior truth of the "language of the body." The Encyclical *Humanae vitae* proclaims the connection between this "truth" and love inseparable.

The Redemption of the Body and the Sacramentality of Marriage

General audience of November 28, 1984.

1. As a whole, the catechesis which I began over four years ago and which I am concluding today can be summed up under the title: "Human love in the divine plan," or more precisely, "The redemption of the body and the sacramentality of marriage." The catechesis can be divided into two parts.

The first part was dedicated to a study of Christ's words, which prove to be suitable for opening the current theme. These words were analyzed at length in the totality of the Gospel text: and following the long-lasting reflection it was fitting to emphasize the three texts that were analyzed right in the first part of the catechesis.

There is first of all the text in which Christ refers to "the beginning" in His discussion with the Pharisees on the unity and indissolubility of marriage (cf. Mt. 19:8; Mk. 10:6-9). Next there are the words spoken by Christ in the Sermon on the Mount concerning "concupiscence" as "adultery committed in the heart" (cf. Mt. 5:28). Finally, there are the words reported by all the synoptic Gospels in which Christ refers to the resurrection of the body in the "other world" (cf. Mt. 22:30; Mk. 12:25; Lk. 20:35).

The second part of the catechesis was dedicated to the analysis of the sacrament based on the Letter to the Ephesians (Eph. 5:22-33) which goes back to the biblical "beginning" of marriage expressed in the words of the Book of Genesis: "...a man leaves his father and mother and clings to his wife, and the two of them become one body" (Gn. 2:24).

The catechesis of the first and second parts repeatedly used the term *"theology of the body."* This is in a certain sense a "working" term. The introduction of the term and the concept of "theology of the body" was necessary to establish the theme, "The redemption of the body and the sacramentality of marriage," on a wider base. In fact, we must immediately note that the term "theology of the body" goes far beyond the content of the reflections that were made. These reflections do not include multiple problems which, with regard to their object, belong to the theology of the body (as, for example, the problem of suffering and death, so important in the biblical message). We must state this clearly. Nonetheless, we must also recognize explicitly that the reflections on the theme, "The redemption of the body and the sacramentality of marriage," can be correctly carried out, from the moment when the light of Revelation touches the reality of the human body (that is, on the basis of the "theology of the body"). This is confirmed, among other ways, by the words of the Book of Genesis: "the two of them become one body," words which were originally and thematically at the basis of our argument.

REFLECTING ON
THE SACRAMENT OF MARRIAGE

2. The reflections on the Sacrament of Marriage were carried out by considering the two dimensions essential to this sacrament (as to every other sacrament), that is, the dimension of the Covenant and grace, and the dimension of sign.

Throughout these two dimensions we continually went back to the reflections on the theology of the body, reflections linked to the key words of Christ. We went back to these reflections also when we took up, at the end of this whole series of catechesis, the analysis of the Encyclical *Humanae vitae*.

The doctrine contained in this document of the Church's modern teaching is organically related to both the sacramentality of marriage and the whole biblical question of the theology of the body, centered on the key words of Christ. In a certain sense we can even say that all the reflections that deal with the "redemption of the body and the sacramentality of marriage" seem to constitute an ample commentary on the doctrine contained in the Encyclical *Humanae vitae*.

This commentary seems quite necessary. In fact, the encyclical, in responding to some questions of today in the field of conjugal and family morality, at the same time also raised other questions, as we know, of a bio-medical nature. But also (and above all) they are of a theological nature; they belong to that sphere of anthropology and theology that we have called "theology of the body."

The reflections we made consist in facing the questions raised with regard to the Encyclical *Humanae vitae*. The reaction that the encyclical aroused confirms the importance and the difficulty of these questions. They are reaffirmed also by later pronouncements of Paul VI where he emphasized the possibility of examining the explanation of Christian truth in this area.

In addition, the Exhortation *Familiaris consortio,* fruit of the 1980 Synod of Bishops on "The Role of the Christian Family," confirms it. The document contains an appeal, directed especially to theologians, to elaborate more completely the biblical and personalistic aspects of the doctrine contained in *Humanae vitae.*

To gather the questions raised by the encyclical means to formulate them and at the same time to search again for the answer to them. The doctrine contained in *Familiaris consortio* requires that both the formulation of the questions and the search for an adequate answer focus on the biblical and personalistic aspects. This doctrine also points out the trend of development of the theology of the body, the direction of the development, and therefore also the direction of its progressive completion and deepening.

BIBLICAL ASPECTS

3. The analysis of the *biblical aspects* speaks of the way to place the doctrine of today's Church on the foundation of Revelation. This is important for the development of theology.

Development, that is, progress in theology, takes place in fact through a continual restudying of the deposit of Revelation.

The rooting of the doctrine proclaimed by the Church in all of Tradition and in divine Revelation itself is always open to questions posed by man and also makes use of the instruments most in keeping with modern science and today's culture. It seems that in this area the intense development of philosophical anthropology (especially the anthropology that rests on ethics) most closely faces the questions raised by the Encyclical *Humanae vitae* regarding theology and especially theological ethics.

The analysis of the *personalistic aspects* of the doctrine contained in this document has an existential significance for establishing what true progress, that is, the development of man, is. In fact, throughout all modern civilization—especially in Western civilization—there is an occult and at the same time an explicit enough tendency to measure this progress on the basis of "things," that is, material goods.

The analysis of the *personalistic aspects* of the Church's doctrine, contained in Paul VI's encyclical, emphasizes a determined appeal to measure man's progress on the basis of the "person," that is, of what is good for man as man—what corresponds to his essential dignity.

The analysis of the *personalistic aspects* leads to the conviction that the encyclical presents as a fundamental problem the viewpoint of man's authentic development; this development in fact is measured to the greatest extent on the basis of ethics and not only on "technology."

"HUMANAE VITAE"

4. The catechesis dedicated to the Encyclical *Humanae vitae* constitutes only one part, the final part, of those which dealt with the redemption of the body and the sacramentality of marriage.

If I draw your attention particularly to this last catechesis, I do so not only because the subject dealt with is more closely connected to our contemporaneity, but above all for the fact that questions come from it that in a certain sense permeate the sum total of our reflections. It follows that this last part is not artificially added to the sum total but is organically and homogeneously united with it. In a certain sense, that part which in the complex arrangement is located at the end is at the same time found at the beginning of this sum total. This is important from the point of view of structure and method.

Even the historical moment seems to have its significance: in fact, the present catechesis was begun in the period of preparation for the

1980 Synod of Bishops on the theme of marriage and the family ("The role of the Christian family"), and ends after the publication of the Exhortation *Familiaris consortio,* which is a result of the work of this Synod. Everyone knows that the 1980 Synod also referred to the Encyclical *Humanae vitae* and fully reconfirmed its doctrine.

Nevertheless, the most important moment seems to be that essential moment when, in the sum total of the reflections carried out, we can precisely state the following: to face the questions raised by the Encyclical *Humanae vitae,* especially in theology, to formulate these questions and seek their reply, it is necessary to find that biblical-theological sphere to which we allude when we speak of "redemption of the body and sacramentality of marriage." In this sphere are found the answers to the perennial questions in the conscience of men and women and also to the difficult questions of our modern world concerning marriage and procreation.

Daughters of St. Paul

MASSACHUSETTS

50 St. Paul's Ave., Jamaica Plain, Boston, MA 02130; **617-522-8911.**

172 Tremont Street, Boston, MA 02111; **617-426-5464; 617-426-4230.**

NEW YORK

78 Fort Place, Staten Island, NY 10301; **718-447-5071; 718-447-5086.**

59 East 43rd Street, New York, NY 10017; **212-986-7580.**

625 East 187th Street, Bronx, NY 10458; **212-584-0440.**

525 Main Street, Buffalo, NY 14203; **716-847-6044.**

NEW JERSEY

Hudson Mall—Route 440 and Communipaw Ave.,
Jersey City, NJ 07304; **201-433-7740.**

CONNECTICUT

202 Fairfield Ave., Bridgeport, CT 06604; **203-335-9913.**

OHIO

2105 Ontario Street (at Prospect Ave.), Cleveland, OH 44115;
216-621-9427.

616 Walnut Street, Cincinnati, OH 45202; **513-421-5733; 513-721-5059.**

PENNSYLVANIA

1719 Chestnut Street, Philadelphia, PA 19103; **215-568-2638.**

VIRGINIA

1025 King Street, Alexandria, VA 22314; **703-683-1741; 703-549-3806.**

SOUTH CAROLINA

243 King Street, Charleston, SC 29401; **803-577-0175.**

FLORIDA

2700 Biscayne Blvd., Miami, FL 33137; **305-573-1618; 305-573-1624.**

LOUISIANA

4403 Veterans Memorial Blvd., Metairie, LA 70006; **504-887-7631;
504-887-0113.**

423 Main Street, Baton Rouge. LA 70802; **504-343-4057; 504-381-9485.**

MISSOURI

1001 Pine Street (at North 10th), St. Louis, MO 63101; **314-621-0346;
314-231-1034.**

ILLINOIS

172 North Michigan Ave., Chicago, IL 60601; **312-346-4228; 312-346-3240.**

TEXAS

114 Main Plaza, San Antonio, TX 78205; **512-224-8101; 512-224-0938.**

CALIFORNIA

1570 Fifth Ave., San Diego, CA 92101; **619-232-1442.**

46 Geary Street, San Francisco, CA 94108; **415-781-5180.**

WASHINGTON

2301 Second Ave., Seattle, WA 98121; **206-441-3300; 206-441-3210.**

HAWAII

1143 Bishop Street, Honolulu, HI 96813; **808-521-2731.**

ALASKA

750 West 5th Ave., Anchorage, AK 99501; **907-272-8183.**

CANADA

3022 Dufferin Street, Toronto 395, Ontario, Canada.